Contents

About
Vocabulary Centers
Grades 2-3

What's Great About This Book

Centers are a wonderful, fun way for students to practice important skills. The 12 centers in this book are self-contained and portable. Students may work at a desk, at a table, or even on the floor. Once you've made the centers, they're ready to use any time.

What's in This Book

Teacher and student directions
include how to make and use the center

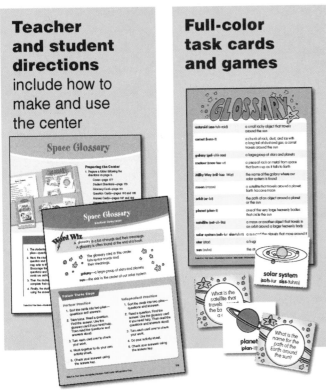

Full-color task cards and games

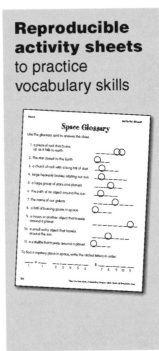

Reproducible activity sheets
to practice vocabulary skills

Self-checking answer keys

How to Use the Centers

The centers are intended for skill practice, not to introduce skills. It is important to model the use of each center before students do the task independently.

Questions to Consider:

- Will students select a center, or will you assign the centers?
- Will there be a specific block of time for centers, or will the centers be used throughout the day?
- Where will you place the centers for easy access by students?
- What procedure will students use when they need help with the center tasks?
- How will you track the tasks and centers completed by each student?

Making a File Folder Center

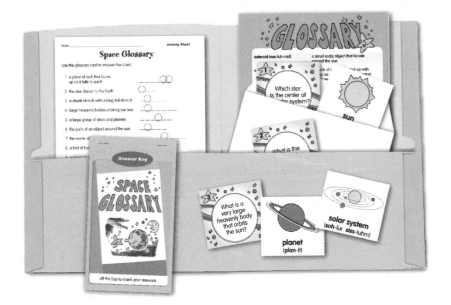

Folder centers are easily stored in a box or file crate. Students take a folder to their desks to complete the task.

Materials:

- folder with pockets
- envelopes
- marking pens and pencils
- scissors
- stapler
- glue or two-sided tape
- paper fasteners

Folder Back

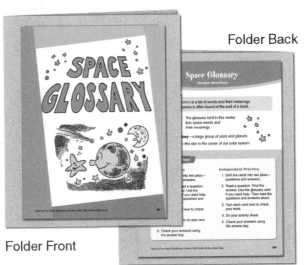

Folder Front

Steps to Follow:

1. Laminate the cover. Tape it to the front of the folder.

2. Laminate the student directions page. Tape it to the back of the folder.

3. Laminate the self-checking answer key for each center. Cut the page in half. Staple the cover on top of the answer key. Place the answer key in the left-hand pocket.

4. Place activity sheets and any other supplies in the left-hand pocket.

5. Laminate the task cards and puzzle pieces. Place each set in a labeled envelope in the right-hand pocket.

6. If needed for a center, laminate the sorting mat or game board and place it in the right-hand pocket of the folder.

Center Checklist

Student Names

Centers

"Ph" Words										
Polygons										
Gr-r-reat Words										
Synonym Circles										
Rhyming Riddles										
More Than One Meaning										
Antonym Action										
How Do You Feel?										
Make a New Word										
Which Suffix?										
Comparisons										
Space Glossary										

"Ph" Words

Preparing the Center

1. Prepare a folder following the directions on page 3.

   Cover—page 7

   Student Directions—page 9

   Puzzle Pieces—pages 11–17

   Answer Key—page 19

2. Reproduce a supply of the activity sheet on page 6. Place copies in the left-hand pocket of the folder.

Partner Practice

1. The students sort the puzzle pieces into three piles—pictures, words, definitions.

2. The students take turns selecting a picture and matching it to its word name and definition. Encourage the students to read the words aloud using the kid-friendly pronunciations.

3. Then the students work cooperatively to complete their own activity sheet.

4. Finally, the students check the answers using the answer key.

Independent Practice

1. The student sorts the puzzle pieces into three piles—pictures, words, definitions.

2. The student selects a picture and matches it to its word name and definition. Encourage the student to read the words aloud using the kid-friendly pronunciations.

3. Then the student completes the activity sheet.

4. Finally, the student self-checks by using the answer key.

"Ph" Words

Read each clue. Find the word in the word box that matches the clue.
Write the missing letters on the lines.

1. p h ____ ____ ____ ____ ____

2. ____ ____ p h ____ ____ ____

3. ____ ____ ____ ____ ____ ____ ____ p h

4. p h ____ ____ ____ ____ ____ ____ ____

5. ____ ____ ____ p h ____ ____ ____

6. ____ p h ____ ____ ____

7. ____ ____ ____ p h ____

8. p h ____ ____ ____ ____ ____

Clues
1. ghost
2. storm
3. written name
4. doctor
5. pencil lead
6. globe
7. award
8. bird

Word Box			
autograph	phantom	physician	trophy
graphite	pheasant	sphere	typhoon

Take It to Your Seat—Vocabulary Centers • EMC 3349 • © Evan-Moor Corp.

Word Wiz

The letters **ph** together stand for the same sound as the letter **f**.

Father took a **photograph** of the **trophy** I won.

photogra**ph**   (**f**oh-tuh-gra**f**)

tro**ph**y   (troh-**f**ee)

Follow These Steps

Partner Practice

1. Sort the puzzle pieces into three piles—pictures, words, and definitions.

2. Take turns putting each puzzle together.

3. Read the words and definitions in each puzzle aloud.

4. Work together to do your own activity sheet.

5. Use the answer key to check your answers.

Independent Practice

1. Sort the puzzle pieces into three piles—pictures, words, and definitions.

2. Put each puzzle together.

3. Read the words and definitions aloud.

4. Do the activity sheet.

5. Use the answer key to check your answers.

photograph
(foh-tuh-graf)

a picture taken
with a camera

physician
(fuh-**zish**-un)

a doctor

pheasant
(**fez**-unt)

a large bird with
a long, slender tail
and beautiful feathers

"Ph" Words

EMC 3349 • © Evan-Moor Corp.

"Ph" Words

EMC 3349 • © Evan-Moor Corp.

"Ph" Words

EMC 3349 • © Evan-Moor Corp.

"Ph" Words

EMC 3349 • © Evan-Moor Corp.

"Ph" Words

EMC 3349 • © Evan-Moor Corp.

"Ph" Words

EMC 3349 • © Evan-Moor Corp.

"Ph" Words

EMC 3349 • © Evan-Moor Corp.

"Ph" Words

EMC 3349 • © Evan-Moor Corp.

phantom
(**fan**-tum)

a ghost

pharaoh
(**fair**-oh)

a name used long ago for rulers of Egypt

trophy
(**troh**-fee)

an award given to a winner

"Ph" Words

EMC 3349 • © Evan-Moor Corp.

"Ph" Words

EMC 3349 • © Evan-Moor Corp.

"Ph" Words

EMC 3349 • © Evan-Moor Corp.

"Ph" Words

EMC 3349 • © Evan-Moor Corp.

"Ph" Words

EMC 3349 • © Evan-Moor Corp.

"Ph" Words

EMC 3349 • © Evan-Moor Corp.

"Ph" Words

EMC 3349 • © Evan-Moor Corp.

"Ph" Words

EMC 3349 • © Evan-Moor Corp.

gopher
(**goh**-fur)

a furry animal that lives underground

sphere
(sfeer)

a solid round shape like a ball or globe

graphite
(**graf**-ite)

the lead in pencils

"Ph" Words
EMC 3349 • © Evan-Moor Corp.

"Ph" Words
EMC 3349 • © Evan-Moor Corp.

"Ph" Words
EMC 3349 • © Evan-Moor Corp.

"Ph" Words
EMC 3349 • © Evan-Moor Corp.

"Ph" Words
EMC 3349 • © Evan-Moor Corp.

"Ph" Words
EMC 3349 • © Evan-Moor Corp.

"Ph" Words
EMC 3349 • © Evan-Moor Corp.

"Ph" Words
EMC 3349 • © Evan-Moor Corp.

"Ph" Words
EMC 3349 • © Evan-Moor Corp.

graph
(graf)

a diagram that shows information

typhoon
(tie-**foon**)

a storm that starts in an ocean or sea; a hurricane

autograph
(**aw**-tuh-graf)

a person's handwritten name

"Ph" Words

EMC 3349 • © Evan-Moor Corp.

"Ph" Words

EMC 3349 • © Evan-Moor Corp.

"Ph" Words

EMC 3349 • © Evan-Moor Corp.

"Ph" Words

EMC 3349 • © Evan-Moor Corp.

"Ph" Words

EMC 3349 • © Evan-Moor Corp.

"Ph" Words

EMC 3349 • © Evan-Moor Corp.

"Ph" Words

EMC 3349 • © Evan-Moor Corp.

"Ph" Words

EMC 3349 • © Evan-Moor Corp.

"Ph" Words

EMC 3349 • © Evan-Moor Corp.

"Ph" Words

1. phantom
2. typhoon
3. autograph
4. physician
5. graphite
6. sphere
7. trophy
8. pheasant

Lift the flap to check your answers.

Polygons

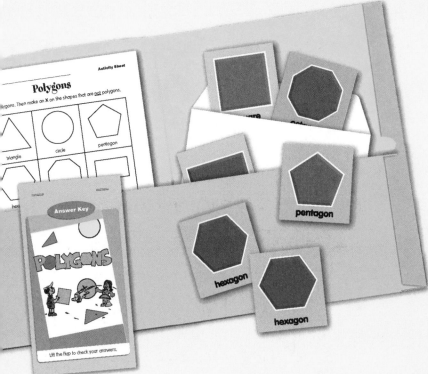

Preparing the Center

1. Prepare a folder following the directions on page 3.

   Cover—page 23

   Student Directions—page 25

   Game Rules—page 27

   Task Cards—pages 29 and 31

   Answer Key—page 33

2. Reproduce a supply of the activity sheet on page 22. Place copies in the left-hand pocket of the folder.

Partner Practice

1. The students read the game rules for two players.

2. The students play the matching game. Encourage the students to read the words aloud.

3. Then the students work cooperatively to complete their own activity sheet.

4. Finally, the students check the answers using the answer key.

Independent Practice

1. The student reads the game rules for one player.

2. The student plays the game, continuing until all matches have been made. Encourage the student to read the words aloud.

3. Then the student completes the activity sheet.

4. Finally, the student self-checks by using the answer key.

Polygons

Color the polygons. Then make an **X** on the shapes that are <u>not</u> polygons.

triangle	circle	pentagon
hexagon	octagon	rectangle
angle	oval	square

Take It to Your Seat—Vocabulary Centers • EMC 3349 • © Evan-Moor Corp.

Word Wiz

A **polygon** is a flat closed figure.
A polygon has three or more straight lines.

A **square** is a polygon.
A square has four straight sides.

A **circle** is <u>not</u> a polygon.
A circle has no straight lines.

Follow These Steps

Partner Practice

1. Read the game rules for two players.

2. Play the matching game.

3. Work together to do your own activity sheet.

4. Use the answer key to check your answers.

Independent Practice

1. Read the game rules for one player.

2. Match all the cards.

3. Do the activity sheet.

4. Use the answer key to check your answers.

26

Rules for 2 Players:

1. Place the cards facedown.

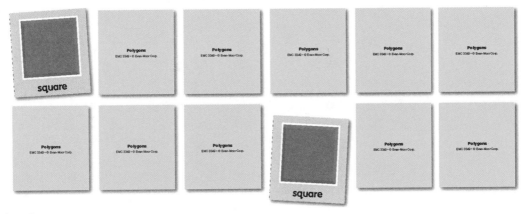

2. Take turns.

3. Turn two cards over. If the cards match, keep them.
   If the cards don't match, turn them back over.

4. After the last match, count your cards.
   The player with the most cards is the winner.

Rules for 1 Player:

1. Place the cards facedown.

2. Turn two cards over.
   If the cards match,
   keep them. If the cards
   don't match, turn them
   back over.

3. Play until you match all
   the cards.

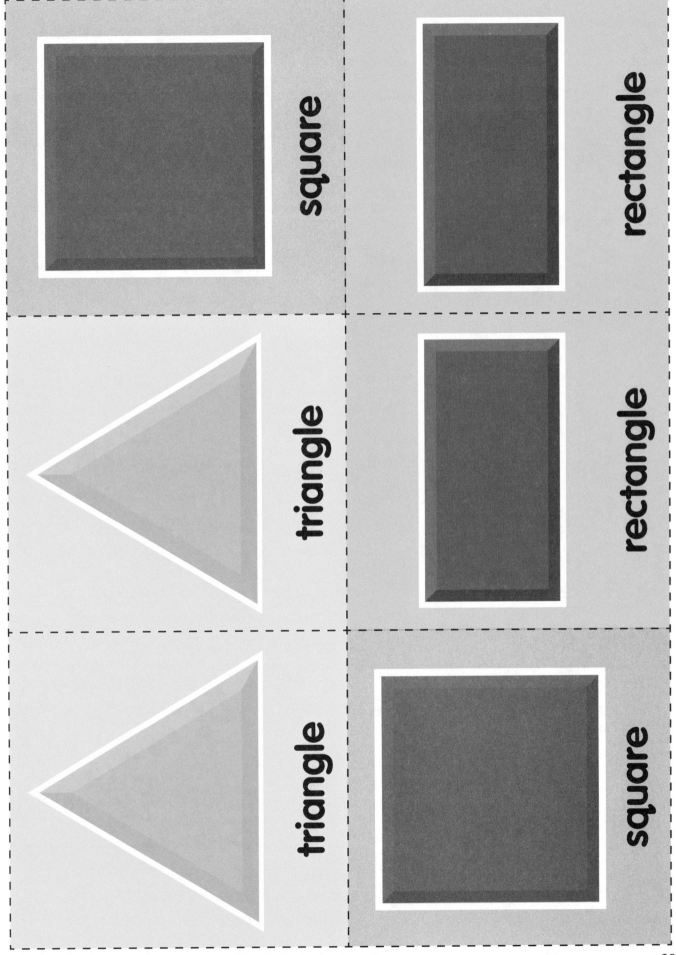

square

rectangle

triangle

rectangle

triangle

square

Polygons

EMC 3349 • © Evan-Moor Corp.

Polygons

EMC 3349 • © Evan-Moor Corp.

Polygons

EMC 3349 • © Evan-Moor Corp.

Polygons

EMC 3349 • © Evan-Moor Corp.

Polygons

EMC 3349 • © Evan-Moor Corp.

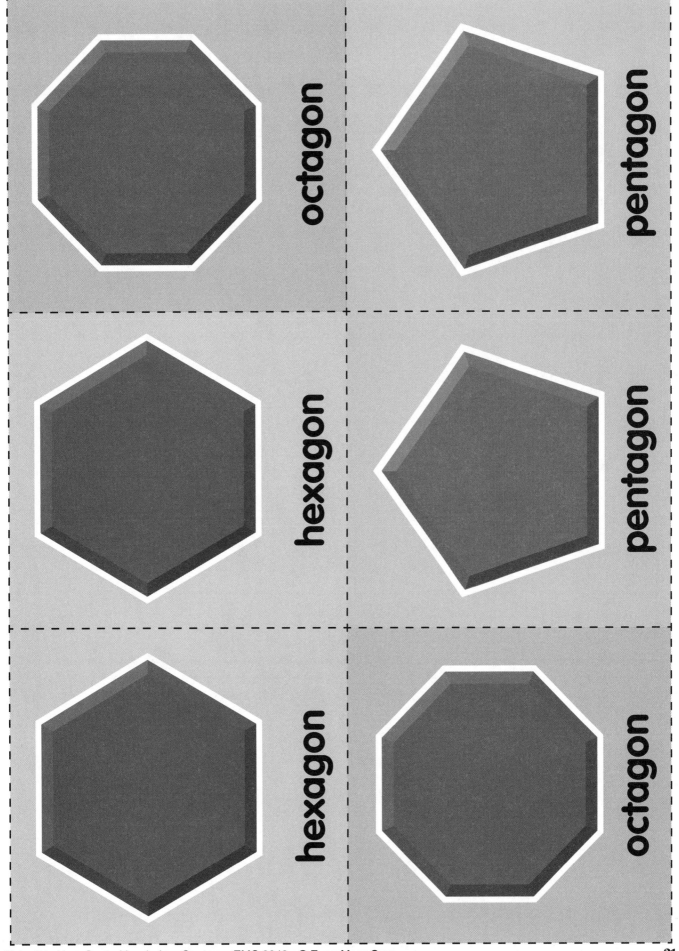

octagon

pentagon

hexagon

pentagon

hexagon

octagon

Polygons

EMC 3349 • © Evan-Moor Corp.

Polygons

EMC 3349 • © Evan-Moor Corp.

Polygons

EMC 3349 • © Evan-Moor Corp.

Polygons

EMC 3349 • © Evan-Moor Corp.

Polygons

EMC 3349 • © Evan-Moor Corp.

Polygons

EMC 3349 • © Evan-Moor Corp.

Polygons

pentagon	circle	triangle
rectangle	octagon	hexagon
square	oval	angle

Answer Key

Lift the flap to check your answers.

Gr-r-reat Words

Preparing the Center

1. Prepare a folder following the directions on page 3.

>   Cover—page 37
>
>   Student Directions—page 39
>
>   Game Rules—page 41
>
>   Game Cards—pages 43–47
>
>   Answer Key—page 49

2. Reproduce a supply of the activity sheet on page 36. Place copies in the left-hand pocket of the folder.

Partner Practice

1. The students read the game rules for two players. They shuffle the *gr* word cards and place them facedown in a pile.

2. The students play the game in the same way as the card game Go Fish. Encourage the students to read the cards aloud as they play.

3. Then the students work cooperatively to complete their own activity sheet.

4. Finally, the students check the answers using the answer key.

Independent Practice

1. The student reads the game rules for one player. The student shuffles the *gr* word cards and places them facedown in rows.

2. The student plays the game in the same way as the game Concentration. Encourage the student to read the cards aloud while playing.

3. Then the student completes the activity sheet.

4. Finally, the student self-checks by using the answer key.

Gr-r-reat Words

Look at each picture.
Circle the adjective that best describes what you see.

greedy   groggy

grateful   greasy

grimy   graceful

gruesome   greasy

grouchy   grateful

groggy   grassy

GR-R-REAT WORDS

"GRASSY"

Word Wiz

An **adjective** is a word that describes.

Greedy is an adjective.

The word **greedy** describes the child.

The **greedy** child took all the cookies.

Follow These Steps

Partner Practice

1. Read the game rules for two players.

2. Play the matching game.

3. Work together to do your own activity sheet.

4. Use the answer key to check your answers.

Independent Practice

1. Read the game rules for one player.

2. Match all the cards.

3. Do the activity sheet.

4. Use the answer key to check your answers.

Gr-r-reat Words

Rules for 2 Players:

1. Shuffle the cards. Place the cards facedown in a pile.

2. Each of you takes 4 cards from the pile. Don't show your cards to the other player.

3. Take turns asking for a card as in the game Go Fish. If the other player has the card you ask for, you get to keep it. This makes a pair. Put the two cards down. If the other player does not have the card, you must take the top card from the pile.

4. After all the matches have been made, count your cards. The player with the most cards is the winner.

Rules for 1 Player:

1. Shuffle the cards. Place the cards facedown in rows.

2. Take any two cards and try to make a match as in the game Concentration. If the cards match, set them aside. If they don't match, turn them back over and try again. See how long it takes you to make all nine matches.

groggy

grimy

greedy

grimy

greedy

groggy

Gr-r-reat Words

EMC 3349 • © Evan-Moor Corp.

Gr-r-reat Words

EMC 3349 • © Evan-Moor Corp.

Gr-r-reat Words

EMC 3349 • © Evan-Moor Corp.

Gr-r-reat Words

EMC 3349 • © Evan-Moor Corp.

Gr-r-reat Words

EMC 3349 • © Evan-Moor Corp.

Gr-r-reat Words

EMC 3349 • © Evan-Moor Corp.

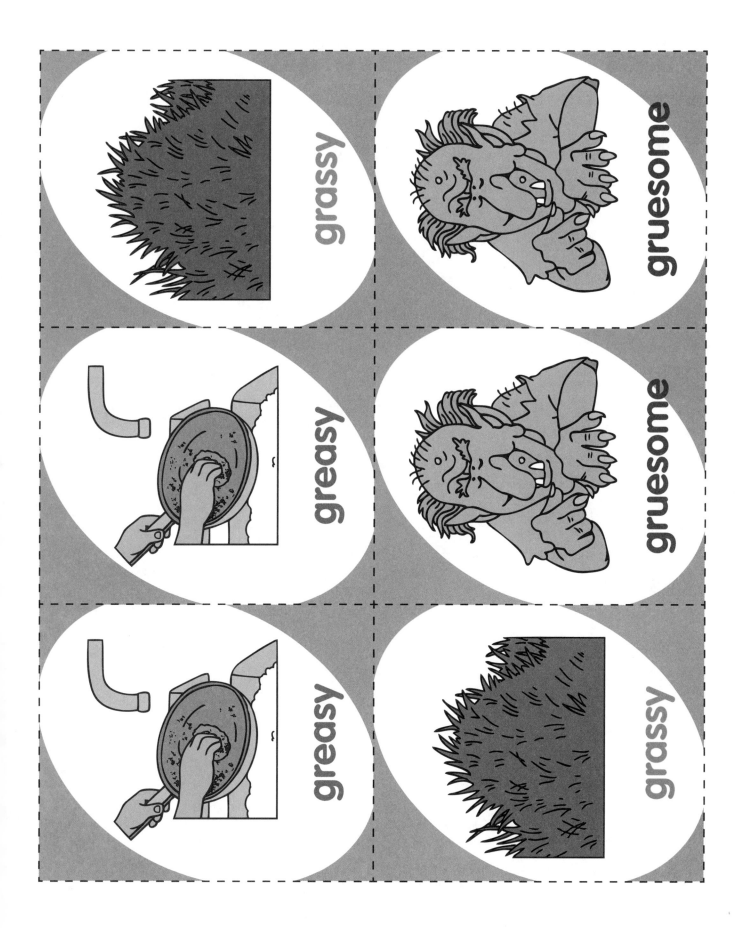

grassy

gruesome

greasy

gruesome

greasy

grassy

Gr-r-reat Words

EMC 3349 • © Evan-Moor Corp.

Gr-r-reat Words

EMC 3349 • © Evan-Moor Corp.

Gr-r-reat Words

EMC 3349 • © Evan-Moor Corp.

Gr-r-reat Words

EMC 3349 • © Evan-Moor Corp.

Gr-r-reat Words

EMC 3349 • © Evan-Moor Corp.

Gr-r-reat Words

EMC 3349 • © Evan-Moor Corp.

grateful

graceful

grouchy

graceful

grouchy

grateful

Gr-r-reat Words

EMC 3349 • © Evan-Moor Corp.

Gr-r-reat Words

EMC 3349 • © Evan-Moor Corp.

Gr-r-reat Words

EMC 3349 • © Evan-Moor Corp.

Gr-r-reat Words

EMC 3349 • © Evan-Moor Corp.

Gr-r-reat Words

EMC 3349 • © Evan-Moor Corp.

Gr-r-reat Words

EMC 3349 • © Evan-Moor Corp.

Gr-r-reat Words

Lift the flap to check your answers.

Synonym Circles

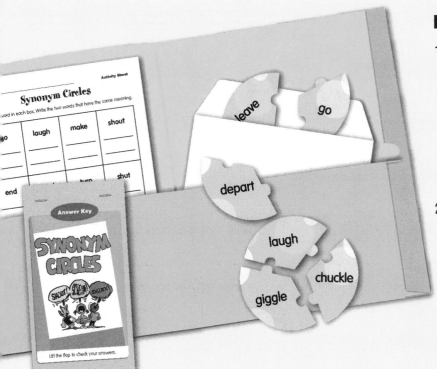

Preparing the Center

1. Prepare a folder following the directions on page 3.

   Cover—page 53

   Student Directions—page 55

   Puzzle Pieces—pages 57–63

   Answer Key—page 65

2. Reproduce a supply of the activity sheet on page 52. Place copies in the left-hand pocket of the folder.

Partner Practice

1. The students take the puzzle pieces.

2. The students work together to find three puzzle pieces with words that have the same meaning. As each puzzle is completed, the students take turns reading the synonyms aloud.

3. Then the students work cooperatively to complete their own activity sheet.

4. Finally, the students check the answers using the answer key.

Independent Practice

1. The student puts together the three puzzle pieces with words that have the same meaning. The student continues until all the puzzles have been completed. Encourage the student to read aloud the synonyms that form each puzzle.

2. Then the student completes the activity sheet.

3. Finally, the student self-checks by using the answer key.

Synonym Circles

Read the word in each box. Write the two words that have the same meaning.

go	laugh	make	shout
_____	_____	_____	_____
_____	_____	_____	_____

end	find	turn	shut
_____	_____	_____	_____
_____	_____	_____	_____

Word Box

build	construct	giggle	scream
chuckle	depart	leave	seal
close	discover	locate	shriek
complete	finish	rotate	twist

SYNONYM CIRCLES

Synonym Circles

Word Wiz

Some words can mean the same thing.
Words that mean the same thing are called **synonyms**.

Leave, **depart**, and **go** are synonyms.

We must **leave** by 6:00.

We must **depart** by 6:00.

We must **go** by 6:00.

Follow These Steps

Partner Practice

1. Take the puzzle pieces.

2. Work together to complete the puzzles. Find the three words that have the same meaning. Read the words aloud.

3. Work together to do your own activity sheet.

4. Check your answers using the answer key.

Independent Practice

1. Take the puzzle pieces.

2. Put the puzzles together. Find the three words that have the same meaning. Read the words aloud.

3. Do the activity sheet.

4. Check your answers using the answer key.

leave

go

depart

laugh

chuckle

giggle

Synonym Circles

EMC 3349 • © Evan-Moor Corp.

Synonym Circles

EMC 3349 • © Evan-Moor Corp.

Synonym Circles

EMC 3349 • © Evan-Moor Corp.

Synonym Circles

EMC 3349 • © Evan-Moor Corp.

Synonym Circles

EMC 3349 • © Evan-Moor Corp.

Synonym Circles

EMC 3349 • © Evan-Moor Corp.

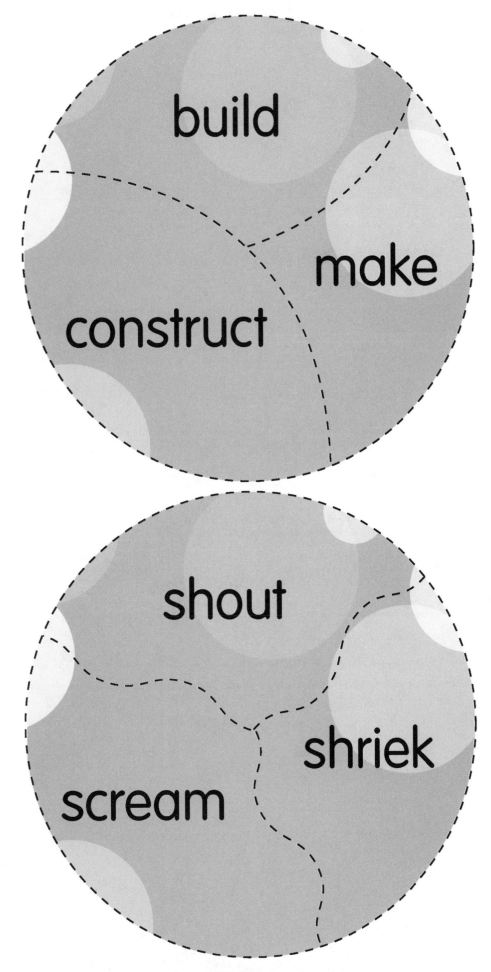

build

make

construct

shout

shriek

scream

Synonym Circles

EMC 3349 • © Evan-Moor Corp.

Synonym Circles

EMC 3349 • © Evan-Moor Corp.

Synonym Circles

EMC 3349 • © Evan-Moor Corp.

Synonym Circles

EMC 3349 • © Evan-Moor Corp.

Synonym Circles

EMC 3349 • © Evan-Moor Corp.

Synonym Circles

EMC 3349 • © Evan-Moor Corp.

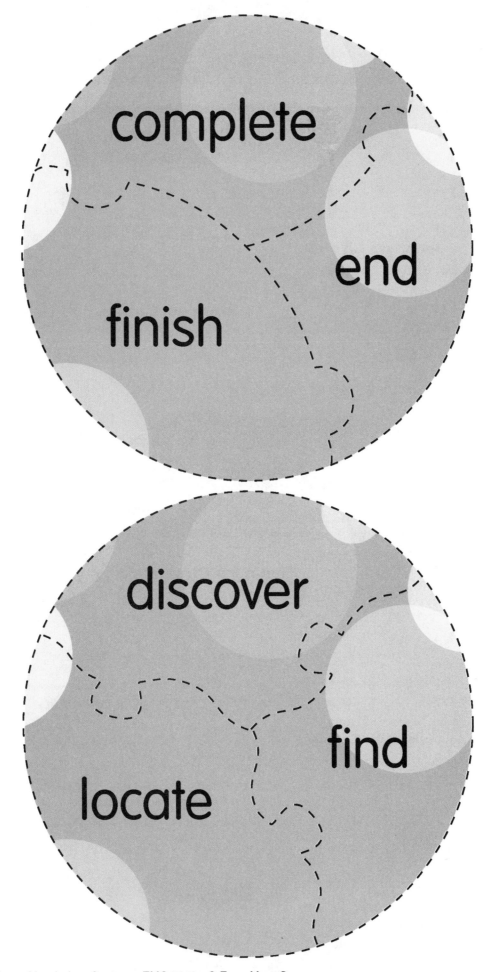

complete

end

finish

discover

find

locate

Synonym Circles

EMC 3349 • © Evan-Moor Corp.

Synonym Circles

EMC 3349 • © Evan-Moor Corp.

Synonym Circles

EMC 3349 • © Evan-Moor Corp.

Synonym Circles

EMC 3349 • © Evan-Moor Corp.

Synonym Circles

EMC 3349 • © Evan-Moor Corp.

Synonym Circles

EMC 3349 • © Evan-Moor Corp.

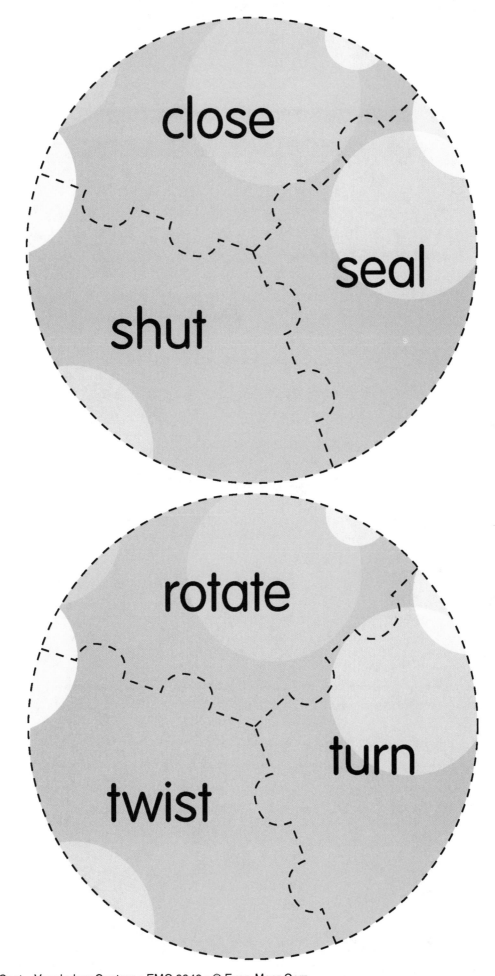

Synonym Circles

EMC 3349 • © Evan-Moor Corp.

Synonym Circles

EMC 3349 • © Evan-Moor Corp.

Synonym Circles

EMC 3349 • © Evan-Moor Corp.

Synonym Circles

EMC 3349 • © Evan-Moor Corp.

Synonym Circles

EMC 3349 • © Evan-Moor Corp.

Synonym Circles

EMC 3349 • © Evan-Moor Corp.

Synonym Circles

shout	make	laugh	go
scream	build	giggle	depart
shriek	construct	chuckle	leave

shut	turn	find	end
close	rotate	locate	complete
seal	twist	discover	finish

Lift the flap to check your answers.

Rhyming Riddles

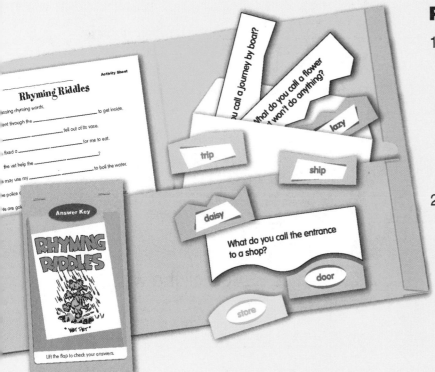

Preparing the Center

1. Prepare a folder following the directions on page 3.

   Cover—page 69

   Student Directions—page 71

   Puzzle Pieces—pages 73–77

   Answer Key—page 79

2. Reproduce a supply of the activity sheet on page 68. Place copies in the left-hand pocket of the folder.

Partner Practice

1. The students place the riddle pieces in a pile and scatter the word pieces faceup.

2. The students take turns reading a riddle and selecting the two rhyming words that answer it. Encourage the students to read aloud each riddle and its answers.

3. Then the students work cooperatively to complete their own activity sheet.

4. Finally, the students check the answers using the answer key.

Independent Practice

1. The student places the riddle pieces in a pile and scatters the word pieces faceup.

2. Next, the student reads a riddle and selects the two rhyming words that answer it. The student continues until all riddles have been answered. Encourage the student to read aloud the riddles and their answers.

3. Then the student completes the activity sheet.

4. Finally, the student self-checks by using the answer key.

Rhyming Riddles

Fill in the missing rhyming words.

1. Max went through the _____ _____ to get inside.

2. The _____ _____ fell out of its vase.

3. Mom fixed a _____ _____ for me to eat.

4. Can the vet help the _____ _____?

5. You may use my _____ _____ to boil the water.

6. The police arrested the _____ _____.

7. We are going on a _____ _____ this summer.

8. Is a mouse the _____ _____ in your house?

9. I tried to get my _____ _____ to laugh.

Word Box		
book	dweller	sad
cellar	frail	ship
crook	kettle	store
dad	lazy	sweet
daisy	metal	treat
door	quail	trip

RHYMING RIDDLES

" WET PET "

Rhyming Riddles

Word Wiz

Words that sound alike are called **rhyming words**.

Candy is a sweet treat.

Sweet and **treat** rhyme.

Follow These Steps

Partner Practice

1. Place the riddle pieces in a pile. Scatter the word pieces faceup.

2. Complete the puzzles. Read a riddle. Find the two rhyming words that answer the riddle. Read the riddles and answers aloud.

3. Work together to do your own activity sheet.

4. Check your answers using the answer key.

Independent Practice

1. Place the riddle pieces in a pile. Scatter the word pieces faceup.

2. Put the puzzles together. Read a riddle. Find the two rhyming words that answer the riddle. Read the riddles and answers aloud.

3. Do the activity sheet.

4. Check your answers using the answer key.

What do you call a journey by boat?

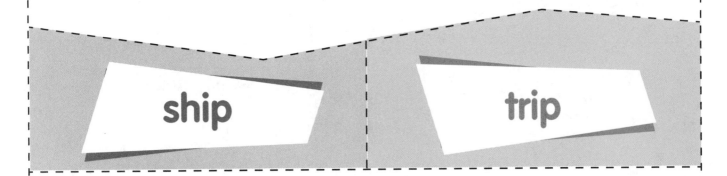

ship   trip

What do you call the entrance to a shop?

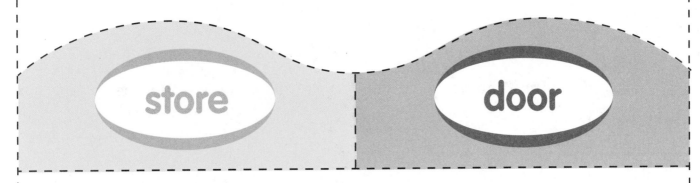

store   door

What do you call a flower that won't do anything?

lazy   daisy

Rhyming Riddles

EMC 3349 • © Evan-Moor Corp.

Rhyming Riddles

EMC 3349 • © Evan-Moor Corp.

Rhyming Riddles

EMC 3349 • © Evan-Moor Corp.

Rhyming Riddles

EMC 3349 • © Evan-Moor Corp.

Rhyming Riddles

EMC 3349 • © Evan-Moor Corp.

Rhyming Riddles

EMC 3349 • © Evan-Moor Corp.

Rhyming Riddles

EMC 3349 • © Evan-Moor Corp.

Rhyming Riddles

EMC 3349 • © Evan-Moor Corp.

Rhyming Riddles

EMC 3349 • © Evan-Moor Corp.

What do you call a sugary snack?

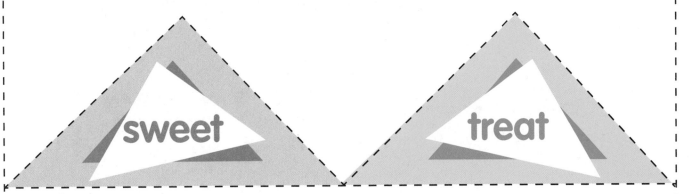

sweet   treat

What do you call a library thief?

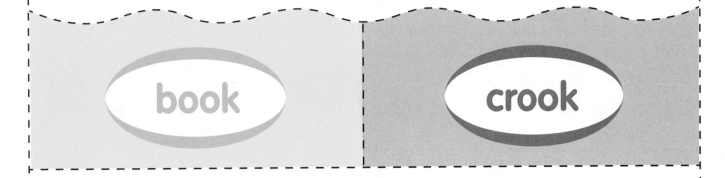

book   crook

What do you call an iron teapot?

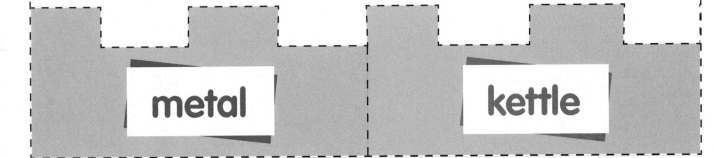

metal   kettle

Rhyming Riddles

EMC 3349 • © Evan-Moor Corp.

Rhyming Riddles

EMC 3349 • © Evan-Moor Corp.

Rhyming Riddles

EMC 3349 • © Evan-Moor Corp.

Rhyming Riddles

EMC 3349 • © Evan-Moor Corp.

Rhyming Riddles

EMC 3349 • © Evan-Moor Corp.

Rhyming Riddles

EMC 3349 • © Evan-Moor Corp.

Rhyming Riddles

EMC 3349 • © Evan-Moor Corp.

Rhyming Riddles

EMC 3349 • © Evan-Moor Corp.

Rhyming Riddles

EMC 3349 • © Evan-Moor Corp.

What do you call a weak bird?

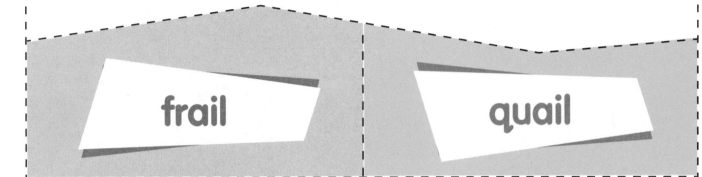

frail

quail

What do you call an unhappy father?

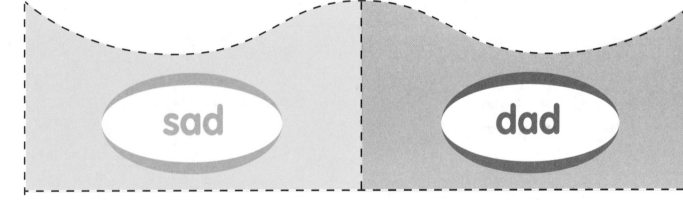

sad

dad

What do you call someone who lives in the basement of a house?

cellar

dweller

Rhyming Riddles

EMC 3349 • © Evan-Moor Corp.

Rhyming Riddles

EMC 3349 • © Evan-Moor Corp.

Rhyming Riddles

EMC 3349 • © Evan-Moor Corp.

Rhyming Riddles

EMC 3349 • © Evan-Moor Corp.

Rhyming Riddles

EMC 3349 • © Evan-Moor Corp.

Rhyming Riddles

EMC 3349 • © Evan-Moor Corp.

Rhyming Riddles

EMC 3349 • © Evan-Moor Corp.

Rhyming Riddles

EMC 3349 • © Evan-Moor Corp.

Rhyming Riddles

EMC 3349 • © Evan-Moor Corp.

Rhyming Riddles

1. store door
2. lazy daisy
3. sweet treat
4. frail quail
5. metal kettle
6. book crook
7. ship trip
8. cellar dweller
9. sad dad

RHYMING RIDDLES

"WET PET"

Lift the flap to check your answers.

More Than One Meaning

Preparing the Center

1. Prepare a folder following the directions on page 3.

   Cover—page 83

   Student Directions—page 85

   Sentence Cards—pages 87–91

   Word Cards—page 93

   Answer Key—page 95

2. Reproduce a supply of the activity sheet on page 82. Place copies in the left-hand pocket of the folder.

Partner Practice

1. The students place the sentences in a pile and scatter the word cards faceup.

2. The students read the top card in the pile and select the word that correctly completes both sentences. The students take turns reading aloud the completed sentences.

3. The students make all possible matches. The cards are self-checking.

4. Then the students work cooperatively to complete their own activity sheet.

5. Finally, the students check the answers using the answer key.

Independent Practice

1. The student places the sentences in a pile and scatters the word cards faceup.

2. The student reads the top card in the pile and selects the word that correctly completes both sentences. The student reads aloud the completed sentences.

3. The student makes all possible matches. The cards are self-checking.

4. Then the student completes the activity sheet.

5. Finally, the student self-checks by using the answer key.

More Than One Meaning

Fill in the missing words. You will use some words twice.

1. Did you put a _____ on the letter?

2. Fill the _____ with ice and grape _____.

3. The gardener will _____ a _____ tree in the yard.

4. Jerome's cat had a _____ of kittens.

5. We gave our dad a _____ for Father's Day.

6. The streets were filled with _____ after the parade.

7. The _____ threw the ball to the batter.

8. Can you _____ a pretty _____ on the present?

9. Don't _____ on the table with your fist.

Word Box		
bow	pitcher	punch
litter	plant	stamp
palm	pound	tie

MORE THAN ONE MEANING

Many common words have more than one meaning.

ball

Cinderella danced with the prince at the **ball**.

Pete threw the **ball** through the basketball hoop.

Follow These Steps

Partner Practice

1. Pile the sentences and scatter the word cards faceup.

2. Take turns picking the top card and reading the two sentences.

3. Find the word that completes both sentences. Read the completed sentences aloud.

4. Turn the cards over to check your work.

5. Work together to do your own activity sheet.

6. Check your answers using the answer key.

Independent Practice

1. Pile the sentences and scatter the word cards faceup.

2. Take the top card in the pile and read the two sentences.

3. Find the word that completes both sentences. Read the completed sentences aloud.

4. Turn the cards over to check your work.

5. Do the activity sheet.

6. Check your answers using the answer key.

I have a blister on the _____ of my hand.

Dad planted a _____ tree in the yard.

She wore a pink _____ in her hair.

Robin Hood shot a _____ and arrow.

Mom made cherry _____ for the party.

Why did you _____ Tom in the back?

More Than One Meaning

EMC 3349 • © Evan-Moor Corp.

More Than One Meaning

EMC 3349 • © Evan-Moor Corp.

More Than One Meaning

EMC 3349 • © Evan-Moor Corp.

Fill the _____ with lemonade.

The _____ threw the ball to the batter.

She bought a _____ of butter.

Use a hammer to _____ in the nail.

Can I help _____ seeds in the garden?

That _____ is starting to bloom.

More Than One Meaning

EMC 3349 • © Evan-Moor Corp.

More Than One Meaning

EMC 3349 • © Evan-Moor Corp.

More Than One Meaning

EMC 3349 • © Evan-Moor Corp.

We gave Dad a _____ for Father's Day.

The game ended in a _____.

Her cat had a _____ of three kittens.

Will you pick up _____ at the beach?

Don't forget to put a _____ on the letter.

It is noisy when you _____ your feet.

More Than One Meaning

EMC 3349 • © Evan-Moor Corp.

More Than One Meaning

EMC 3349 • © Evan-Moor Corp.

More Than One Meaning

EMC 3349 • © Evan-Moor Corp.

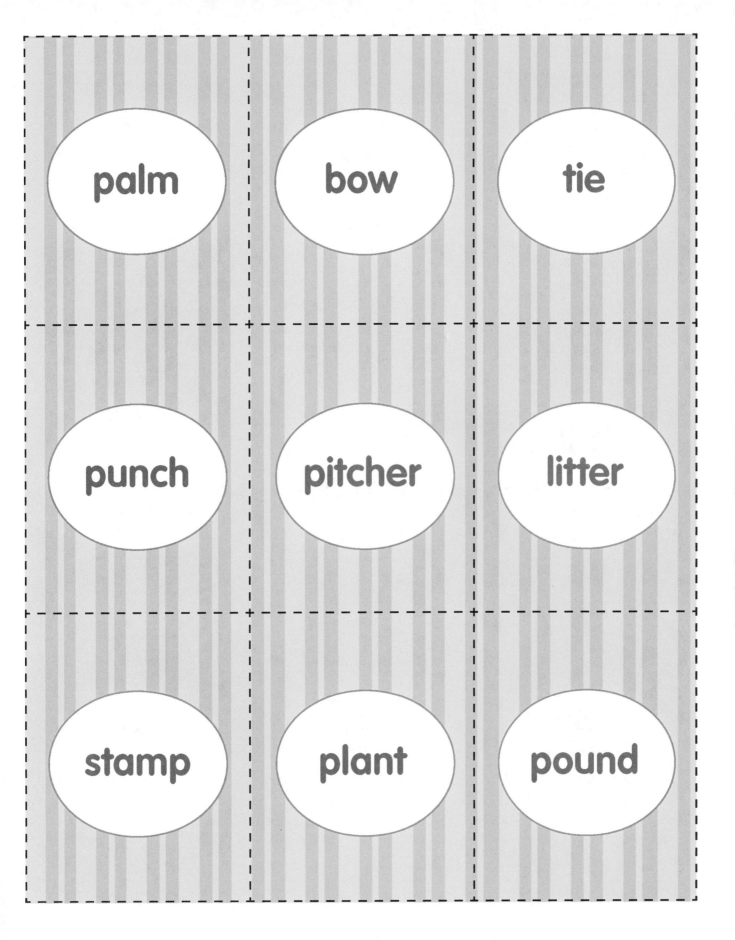

palm

bow

tie

punch

pitcher

litter

stamp

plant

pound

More Than One Meaning

EMC 3349 • © Evan-Moor Corp.

More Than One Meaning

EMC 3349 • © Evan-Moor Corp.

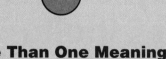

More Than One Meaning

EMC 3349 • © Evan-Moor Corp.

More Than One Meaning

EMC 3349 • © Evan-Moor Corp.

More Than One Meaning

EMC 3349 • © Evan-Moor Corp.

More Than One Meaning

EMC 3349 • © Evan-Moor Corp.

More Than One Meaning

EMC 3349 • © Evan-Moor Corp.

More Than One Meaning

EMC 3349 • © Evan-Moor Corp.

More Than One Meaning

EMC 3349 • © Evan-Moor Corp.

More Than One Meaning

1. stamp

2. pitcher punch

3. plant palm

4. litter

5. tie

6. litter

7. pitcher

8. tie bow

9. pound

MORE THAN ONE MEANING

Lift the flap to check your answers.

Antonym Action

Preparing the Center

1. Prepare a folder following the directions on page 3.

   Cover—page 99

   Student Directions—page 101

   Puzzle Pieces—pages 103–109

   Answer Key—page 111

2. Reproduce a supply of the activity sheet on page 98. Place copies in the left-hand pocket of the folder.

Partner Practice

1. The students sort the puzzle pieces by color into two sets—green and gold.

2. Working together, the students match two antonyms to complete a puzzle. Encourage the students to identify each antonym pair in a sentence such as, "*Smile* and *frown* are antonyms" or "*Smile* and *frown* mean the opposite."

3. Then the students work cooperatively to complete their own activity sheet.

4. Finally, the students check the answers using the answer key.

Independent Practice

1. The student sorts the puzzle pieces by color into two sets—green and gold.

2. The student matches two antonyms to complete each puzzle. Encourage the student to identify each antonym pair in a sentence.

3. Then the student completes the activity sheet.

4. Finally, the student self-checks by using the answer key.

Antonym Action

Read each sentence. Write a word from the box that is an antonym of the word in bold letters.

1. After you eat, your **empty** stomach feels _____.

2. That **giant** flower began as a _____ seed.

3. My **loose** T-shirt was washed and is now too _____.

4. A cat can see in **bright** light as well as in _____ light.

5. Seeing her grandmother made Meghan's **frown** turn into

   a _____.

6. Do you **whisper** on your cell phone or do you _____?

7. **Enter** the bus through the front door and _____ out
   the back.

8. Be careful not to **break** that toy, because it is hard to _____.

9. Do you want **part** of that candy bar, or do you want the

   _____ thing?

10. Once you **start,** how long will it take you to _____ the test?

Word Box				
dim	finish	repair	smile	tiny
exit	full	shout	tight	whole

Take It to Your Seat—Vocabulary Centers • EMC 3349 • © Evan-Moor Corp.

ANTONYM ACTION

Antonym Action

Word Wiz

Some words have the opposite meaning.
Words that have opposite meanings are called antonyms.

Smile and frown mean the opposite.

Smile and frown are antonyms.

smile

frown

Follow These Steps

Partner Practice

1. Sort the puzzle pieces. Put the green pieces in one set. Put the gold pieces in another set.

2. Work together to match a green card with a gold card that has the opposite meaning. Read the opposites aloud.

3. Match all the puzzles.

4. Work together to do your own activity sheet.

5. Use the answer key to check your answers.

Independent Practice

1. Sort the puzzle pieces. Put the green pieces in one set. Put the gold pieces in another set.

2. Match a green card with a gold card that has the opposite meaning. Read the opposites aloud.

3. Match all the puzzles.

4. Do the activity sheet.

5. Check your answers using the answer key.

open

close

full

empty

smile

frown

Antonym Action
EMC 3349 • © Evan-Moor Corp.

Antonym Action
EMC 3349 • © Evan-Moor Corp.

Antonym Action
EMC 3349 • © Evan-Moor Corp.

Antonym Action
EMC 3349 • © Evan-Moor Corp.

Antonym Action
EMC 3349 • © Evan-Moor Corp.

Antonym Action
EMC 3349 • © Evan-Moor Corp.

shout

whisper

dim

bright

loose

tight

Antonym Action

EMC 3349 • © Evan-Moor Corp.

Antonym Action

EMC 3349 • © Evan-Moor Corp.

Antonym Action

EMC 3349 • © Evan-Moor Corp.

Antonym Action

EMC 3349 • © Evan-Moor Corp.

Antonym Action

EMC 3349 • © Evan-Moor Corp.

Antonym Action

EMC 3349 • © Evan-Moor Corp.

enter

exit

giant

tiny

break

repair

Antonym Action

EMC 3349 • © Evan-Moor Corp.

Antonym Action

EMC 3349 • © Evan-Moor Corp.

Antonym Action

EMC 3349 • © Evan-Moor Corp.

Antonym Action

EMC 3349 • © Evan-Moor Corp.

Antonym Action

EMC 3349 • © Evan-Moor Corp.

Antonym Action

EMC 3349 • © Evan-Moor Corp.

sunrise

sunset

part

whole

start

finish

Antonym Action

EMC 3349 • © Evan-Moor Corp.

Antonym Action

EMC 3349 • © Evan-Moor Corp.

Antonym Action

EMC 3349 • © Evan-Moor Corp.

Antonym Action

EMC 3349 • © Evan-Moor Corp.

Antonym Action

EMC 3349 • © Evan-Moor Corp.

Antonym Action

EMC 3349 • © Evan-Moor Corp.

Antonym Action

1. full

2. tiny

3. tight

4. dim

5. smile

6. shout

7. exit

8. repair

9. whole

10. finish

ANTONYM ACTION

Lift the flap to check your answers.

How Do You Feel?

Preparing the Center

1. Prepare a folder following the directions on page 3.

   Cover—page 115

   Student Directions—page 117

   Game Rules—page 119

   Spinner—page 121

   Game Boards—pages 123 and 125

   Word Cards—page 127

   Answer Key—page 129

2. Reproduce a supply of the activity sheet on page 114. Place copies in the left-hand pocket of the folder.

Partner Practice

1. The students read the game rules for two players. They place the word cards faceup. Each student takes a game board.

2. The students follow the rules to play the game. The cards are self-checking.

3. Then the students work cooperatively to complete their own activity sheet.

4. Finally, the students check the answers using the answer key.

Independent Practice

1. The student places the word cards faceup and takes the spinner and a game board.

2. Next, the student reads the rules for one player. The student plays the game until the game board is filled. The cards are self-checking.

3. Then the student completes the activity sheet.

4. Finally, the student self-checks by using the answer key.

How Do You Feel?

Circle the word that correctly completes each sentence.

1. The **(angry, cheerful)** clown made everyone laugh.

2. The **(frightened, sleepy)** child screamed when she saw a bat.

3. Lizzie was **(proud, shy)** of winning a trophy.

4. When Vic saw the confusing map, he was **(frightened, puzzled)**.

5. Yuki felt **(shy, sad)** when she read her book report in front of the class.

6. Ms. Evanston was **(angry, proud)** to see that her new window was broken.

7. Mr. Lee yawned because he was so **(sad, sleepy)**.

8. Keisha was happy and **(frightened, surprised)** when she opened the box.

9. Mike was **(sad, proud)** when his dog ran away.

Word Wiz

Some words describe things or people.
Words that describe things or people are called adjectives.

Frightened, proud, and puzzled are adjectives.

The **frightened** puppy hid under the bed.

The **proud** girl showed her prize to her friends.

The **puzzled** boy asked his teacher for help.

Follow These Steps

Partner Practice

1. Take the rules card, spinner, word cards, and game boards.

2. Place the cards faceup.

3. Read the game rules for two players.

4. Play the game.

5. Work together to do your own activity sheet.

6. Use the answer key to check your answers.

Independent Practice

1. Take the rules card, spinner, word cards, and one game board.

2. Place the cards faceup.

3. Read the game rules for one player.

4. Play the game.

5. Do the activity sheet.

6. Use the answer key to check your answers.

HOW DO YOU FEEL?

Rules for 2 Players:

Take turns following these rules.

1. Spin the spinner.

2. Find the word card that matches the word pointed to by the arrow.

3. Read the word aloud.

4. Place the card on the correct picture on your game board. If you already have a card in that space, you lose that turn.

5. Turn the card over to check your work.

6. Play until one of you fills your board.

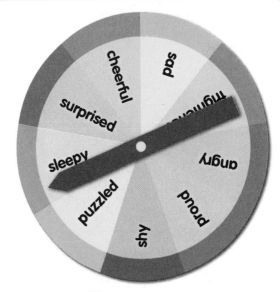

Rules for 1 Player:

1. Spin the spinner.

2. Find the word card that matches the word pointed to by the arrow.

3. Place the card on the correct picture on the game board.

4. Turn the card over to check your work.

5. Play until you fill your board.

Use a paper fastener to attach the arrow to the spinner.

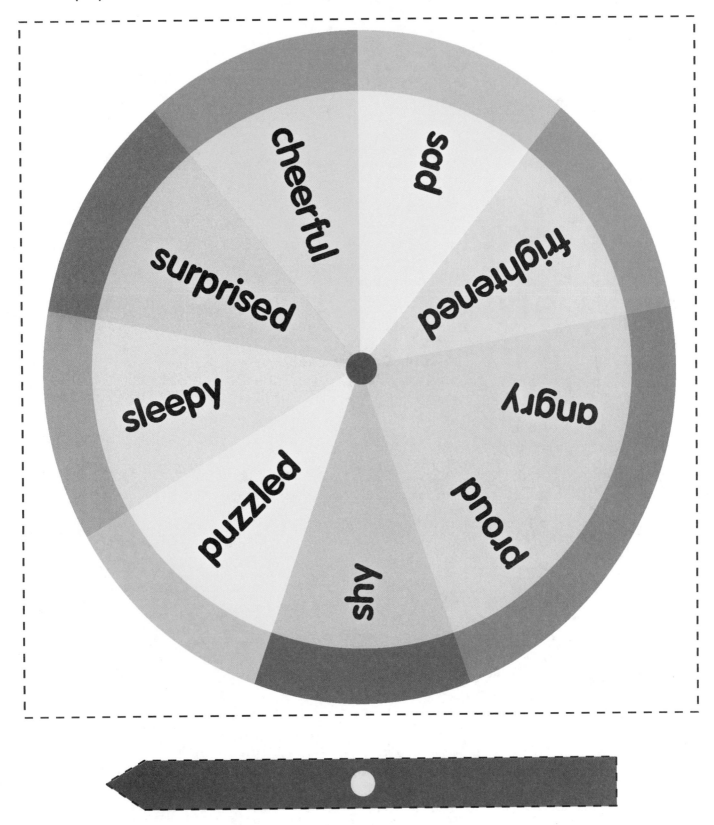

How Do You Feel?

EMC 3349 • © Evan-Moor Corp.

How Do You Feel?

EMC 3349 • © Evan-Moor Corp.

HOW DO YOU FEEL?

HOW DO YOU FEEL?

cheerful	cheerful	sad
sad	frightened	frightened
angry	angry	proud
proud	shy	shy
puzzled	puzzled	sleepy
sleepy	surprised	surprised

How Do You Feel?

EMC 3349 • © Evan-Moor Corp.

How Do You Feel?

EMC 3349 • © Evan-Moor Corp.

How Do You Feel?

EMC 3349 • © Evan-Moor Corp.

How Do You Feel?

EMC 3349 • © Evan-Moor Corp.

How Do You Feel?

EMC 3349 • © Evan-Moor Corp.

How Do You Feel?

EMC 3349 • © Evan-Moor Corp.

How Do You Feel?

EMC 3349 • © Evan-Moor Corp.

How Do You Feel?

EMC 3349 • © Evan-Moor Corp.

How Do You Feel?

EMC 3349 • © Evan-Moor Corp.

How Do You Feel?

EMC 3349 • © Evan-Moor Corp.

How Do You Feel?

EMC 3349 • © Evan-Moor Corp.

How Do You Feel?

EMC 3349 • © Evan-Moor Corp.

How Do You Feel?

EMC 3349 • © Evan-Moor Corp.

How Do You Feel?

EMC 3349 • © Evan-Moor Corp.

How Do You Feel?

EMC 3349 • © Evan-Moor Corp.

How Do You Feel?

EMC 3349 • © Evan-Moor Corp.

How Do You Feel?

EMC 3349 • © Evan-Moor Corp.

How Do You Feel?

EMC 3349 • © Evan-Moor Corp.

How Do You Feel?

1. cheerful

2. frightened

3. proud

4. puzzled

5. shy

6. angry

7. sleepy

8. surprised

9. sad

Lift the flap to check your answers.

Make a New Word

Preparing the Center

1. Prepare a folder following the directions on page 3.

   Cover—page 133

   Student Directions—page 135

   Task Cards—pages 137 and 139

   Answer Key—page 141

2. Reproduce a supply of the activity sheet on page 132. Place copies in the left-hand pocket of the folder.

Partner Practice

1. The students sort the cards into three piles—prefixes, base words, and sentences.

2. The students work together to add prefixes to base words to make new words.

3. Next, the students match each new word to the sentence it completes. Encourage the students to read each completed sentence aloud.

4. Then the students work cooperatively to complete their own activity sheet.

5. Finally, the students check the answers using the answer key.

Independent Practice

1. The student sorts the cards into three piles—prefixes, base words, and sentences.

2. The student adds prefixes to base words to make new words.

3. Next, the student matches each new word to the sentence it completes. Encourage the student to read the completed sentences aloud.

4. Then the student completes the activity sheet.

5. Finally, the student self-checks by using the answer key.

Make a New Word

Complete the sentences. Add the prefix **un** or **re** to make a new word.

1. Mr. Brown didn't _____ pay the money he owed.

2. The naughty boy was _____ kind to his puppy.

3. It makes me _____ happy to fight with my best friend.

4. Dad had to _____ wash the car after the rainstorm.

5. Don't be messy or you will have to _____ write your story.

6. We watched Jimmy _____ paint the doghouse.

7. My little sister is _____ able to tie her own shoes.

8. It is _____ safe to play with fire.

MAKE A NEW WORD

"UNHAPPY"

"HAPPY"

Make a New Word

Word Wiz

A prefix is a word part added to the beginning of a word.
A prefix changes the meaning of the word.

Here are two prefixes: un and re

un means not

un + clear = unclear

Unclear means "not clear."

re means to do again

re + stack = restack

Restack means "to stack again."

Follow These Steps

Partner Practice

1. Sort the cards into three piles—prefixes, base words, and sentences.

2. Work together to add prefixes to words to make new words.

3. Match each new word to the sentence it completes. Take turns reading each sentence aloud.

4. Work together to do your own activity sheet.

5. Use the answer key to check your answers.

Independent Practice

1. Sort the cards into three piles—prefixes, base words, and sentences.

2. Add prefixes to words to make new words.

3. Match each new word to the sentence it completes. Read each sentence aloud.

4. Do the activity sheet.

5. Use the answer key to check your answers.

re pay

Did you _____ the money you owe?

re wash

Go _____ your hands because they are still dirty.

re write

My teacher told me to _____ my story.

re paint

Mom wants to _____ that old chair.

Make a New Word

EMC 3349 • © Evan-Moor Corp.

Make a New Word

EMC 3349 • © Evan-Moor Corp.

Make a New Word

EMC 3349 • © Evan-Moor Corp.

Make a New Word

EMC 3349 • © Evan-Moor Corp.

Make a New Word

EMC 3349 • © Evan-Moor Corp.

Make a New Word

EMC 3349 • © Evan-Moor Corp.

Make a New Word

EMC 3349 • © Evan-Moor Corp.

Make a New Word

EMC 3349 • © Evan-Moor Corp.

Make a New Word

EMC 3349 • © Evan-Moor Corp.

Make a New Word

EMC 3349 • © Evan-Moor Corp.

Make a New Word

EMC 3349 • © Evan-Moor Corp.

Make a New Word

EMC 3349 • © Evan-Moor Corp.

un safe

It is _____ to ride a bike if you do not wear a helmet.

un happy

Sam felt _____ when his dog ran away.

un able

Meg broke her arm and is _____ to play.

un kind

Is it _____ to hit people?

Make a New Word

EMC 3349 • © Evan-Moor Corp.

Make a New Word

EMC 3349 • © Evan-Moor Corp.

Make a New Word

EMC 3349 • © Evan-Moor Corp.

Make a New Word

EMC 3349 • © Evan-Moor Corp.

Make a New Word

EMC 3349 • © Evan-Moor Corp.

Make a New Word

EMC 3349 • © Evan-Moor Corp.

Make a New Word

EMC 3349 • © Evan-Moor Corp.

Make a New Word

EMC 3349 • © Evan-Moor Corp.

Make a New Word

EMC 3349 • © Evan-Moor Corp.

Make a New Word

EMC 3349 • © Evan-Moor Corp.

Make a New Word

1. re
2. un
3. un
4. re
5. re
6. re
7. un
8. un

MAKE A NEW WORD

"HAPPY"

"UNHAPPY"

Lift the flap to check your answers.

Comparisons

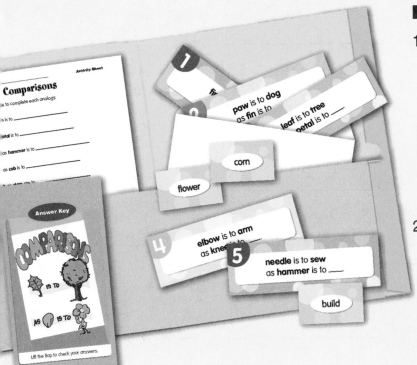

Preparing the Center

1. Prepare a folder following the directions on page 3.

   Cover—page 163

   Student Directions—page 165

   Analogy Cards—pages 167 and 169

   Word Cards—page 171

   Answer Key—page 173

2. Reproduce a supply of the activity sheet on page 162. Place copies in the left-hand pocket of the folder.

Partner Practice

1. The students place the cards faceup in two piles—analogy cards and word cards.

2. Next, the students work together to match a word card with the analogy it completes. Encourage the students to read aloud each completed analogy. The cards are self-checking.

3. Then the students work cooperatively to complete their own activity sheet.

4. Finally, the students check the answers using the answer key.

Independent Practice

1. The student places the cards faceup in two piles—analogy cards and word cards.

2. Next, the student matches a word card with the analogy it completes. Encourage the student to read aloud each completed analogy. The cards are self-checking.

3. Then the student completes the activity sheet.

4. Finally, the student self-checks by using the answer key.

Comparisons

Use a word from the box to complete each analogy.

1. **paw** is to **dog** as **fin** is to _____

2. **leaf** is to **tree** as **petal** is to _____

3. **needle** is to **sew** as **hammer** is to _____

4. **core** is to **apple** as **cob** is to _____

5. **sand** is to **beach** as **stars** are to _____

6. **finger** is to **hand** as **toe** is to _____

7. **peel** is to **banana** as **bark** is to _____

8. **elbow** is to **arm** as **knee** is to _____

Word Box			
build	fish	foot	sky
corn	flower	leg	tree

Word Wiz

An **analogy** is one kind of comparison. An analogy tells what is the same about one set of objects as another set of objects.

This analogy compares one body part to another body part.

wrist is to **hand** as **ankle** is to **foot**

A **wrist** is part of a **hand** in the way an **ankle** is part of a **foot**.

Follow These Steps

Partner Practice

1. Place the cards faceup in two piles—analogies and words.

2. Work together. Read an analogy card. Choose the word that makes the correct comparison. Read each analogy aloud.

3. Turn the word cards over to check your work.

4. Work together to do your own activity sheet.

5. Check your answers using the answer key.

Independent Practice

1. Place the cards faceup in two piles—analogies and words.

2. Read an analogy card. Choose the word that makes the correct comparison. Read each analogy aloud.

3. Turn the word cards over to check your work.

4. Do the activity sheet.

5. Check your answers using the answer key.

1

finger is to **hand** as **toe** is to ____

2

paw is to **dog** as **fin** is to ____

3

leaf is to **tree** as **petal** is to ____

4

elbow is to **arm** as **knee** is to ____

Comparisons

EMC 3349 • © Evan-Moor Corp.

Comparisons

EMC 3349 • © Evan-Moor Corp.

Comparisons

EMC 3349 • © Evan-Moor Corp.

Comparisons

EMC 3349 • © Evan-Moor Corp.

5 needle is to sew
as hammer is to ____

6 core is to apple
as cob is to ____

7 peel is to banana
as bark is to ____

8 sand is to beach
as stars are to ____

Comparisons

EMC 3349 • © Evan-Moor Corp.

Comparisons

EMC 3349 • © Evan-Moor Corp.

Comparisons

EMC 3349 • © Evan-Moor Corp.

Comparisons

EMC 3349 • © Evan-Moor Corp.

foot

corn

fish

flower

sky

build

leg

tree

6

Comparisons

EMC 3349 • © Evan-Moor Corp.

1

Comparisons

EMC 3349 • © Evan-Moor Corp.

3

Comparisons

EMC 3349 • © Evan-Moor Corp.

2

Comparisons

EMC 3349 • © Evan-Moor Corp.

5

Comparisons

EMC 3349 • © Evan-Moor Corp.

8

Comparisons

EMC 3349 • © Evan-Moor Corp.

7

Comparisons

EMC 3349 • © Evan-Moor Corp..

4

Comparisons

EMC 3349 • © Evan-Moor Corp.

Comparisons

1. fish
2. flower
3. build
4. corn
5. sky
6. foot
7. tree
8. leg

COMPARISONS

IS TO

IS TO

AS

Lift the flap to check your answers.

Space Glossary

Preparing the Center

1. Prepare a folder following the directions on page 3.

   > Cover—page 177
   >
   > Student Directions—page 179
   >
   > Glossary Card—page 181
   >
   > Question Cards—pages 183 and 185
   >
   > Answer Cards—pages 187 and 189
   >
   > Answer Key—page 191

2. Reproduce a supply of the activity sheet on page 176. Place copies in the left-hand pocket of the folder.

Partner Practice	Independent Practice
1. The students sort the cards into two piles—questions and answers.	1. The student sorts the cards into two piles—questions and answers.
2. Next, the students take turns reading a question and finding the answer. They may refer to the glossary card for help. Encourage the students to read the questions and answers aloud. The cards are self-checking.	2. Next, the student reads a question and finds the answer. The student may refer to the glossary card for help. Encourage the student to read the questions and answers aloud. The cards are self-checking.
3. Then the students work cooperatively to complete their own activity sheet.	3. Then the student completes the activity sheet.
4. Finally, the students check the answers using the answer key.	4. Finally, the student self-checks by using the answer key.

Space Glossary

Use the glossary card to answer the clues.

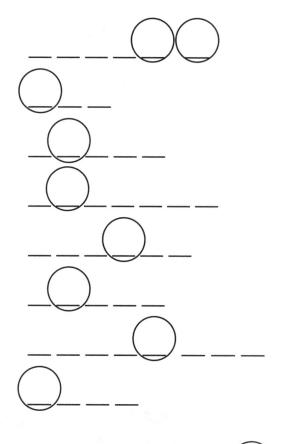

1. a piece of rock that burns up as it falls
   to Earth

2. the star closest to the Earth

3. a chunk of rock with a long tail of dust

4. large heavenly bodies orbiting our sun

5. a large group of stars and planets

6. the path of an object around the sun

7. the name of our galaxy

8. a ball of burning gases in space

9. a moon or another object that travels
   around a planet

10. a small rocky object that travels
    around the sun

11. a satellite that travels around a planet

To find a mystery place in space, write the circled letters in order.

___ u ___   ___ ___ ___ ___ ___   S ___ ___ ___ ___ ___
 1   1   2   3   4   5   6   7   8   9 10 11

SPACE GLOSSARY

Space Glossary

Word Wiz

A **glossary** is a list of words and their meanings. A glossary is often found at the end of a book.

The glossary card in this center lists space words and their meanings.

galaxy—a large group of stars and planets

sun—the star in the center of our solar system

Follow These Steps

Partner Practice

1. Sort the cards into two piles—questions and answers.

2. Take turns. Read a question. Find the answer. Use the glossary card if you need help. Then read the questions and answers aloud.

3. Turn each card over to check your work.

4. Work together to do your own activity sheet.

5. Check your answers using the answer key.

Independent Practice

1. Sort the cards into two piles—questions and answers.

2. Read a question. Find the answer. Use the glossary card if you need help. Then read the questions and answers aloud.

3. Turn each card over to check your work.

4. Do the activity sheet.

5. Check your answers using the answer key.

GLOSSARY

asteroid (**ass**-tuh-roid)   a small rocky object that travels around the sun

comet (**kom**-it)   a chunk of rock, dust, and ice with a long tail of dust and gas; a comet travels around the sun

galaxy (**gal**-uhk-see)   a large group of stars and planets

meteor (**mee**-tee-ur)   a piece of rock or metal from space that burns up as it falls to Earth

Milky Way (**Mil**-kee Way)   the name of the galaxy where our solar system is found

moon (moon)   a satellite that travels around a planet; Earth has one moon

orbit (**or**-bit)   the path of an object around a planet or the sun

planet (**plan**-it)   one of the very large heavenly bodies that circle the sun

satellite (**sat**-uh-lite)   a moon or another object that travels in an orbit around a larger heavenly body

solar system (**soh**-lur **siss**-tuhm)   a sun and the planets that move around it

star (star)   a huge ball of burning gas in space

sun (suhn)   the star in the center of our solar system

1 Which star is the center of our solar system?

2 What is the name of our galaxy?

3 What is a very large heavenly body that orbits the sun?

4 What do we call a ball of burning gas in the sky?

5 What is the name for a sun and the planets that move around it?

6 What is the name for a large group of stars and planets?

Space Glossary

EMC 3349 • © Evan-Moor Corp.

Space Glossary

EMC 3349 • © Evan-Moor Corp.

Space Glossary

EMC 3349 • © Evan-Moor Corp.

Space Glossary

EMC 3349 • © Evan-Moor Corp.

Space Glossary

EMC 3349 • © Evan-Moor Corp.

Space Glossary

EMC 3349 • © Evan-Moor Corp.

7

What is the satellite that travels around the Earth once a day?

8

What is the name for the path of the Earth around the sun?

9

What is another name for a moon?

10

What is a piece of rock or metal from space that burns up as it falls to Earth?

11

What is the name for an object in space with a long tail of dust and gas?

12

What is the name for a small solid object that travels around the sun?

Space Glossary

EMC 3349 • © Evan-Moor Corp.

Space Glossary

EMC 3349 • © Evan-Moor Corp.

Space Glossary

EMC 3349 • © Evan-Moor Corp.

Space Glossary

EMC 3349 • © Evan-Moor Corp.

Space Glossary

EMC 3349 • © Evan-Moor Corp.

Space Glossary

EMC 3349 • © Evan-Moor Corp.

sun
(suhn)

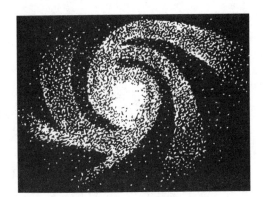

Milky Way
(**Mil**-kee Way)

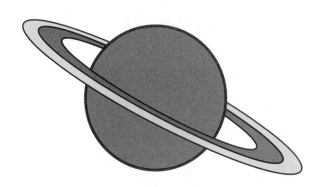

planet
(**plan**-it)

star
(star)

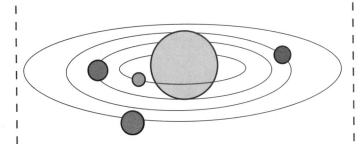

solar system
(**soh**-lur **siss**-tuhm)

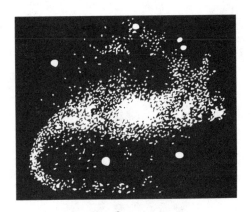

galaxy
(**gal**-uhk-see)

2

Space Glossary

EMC 3349 • © Evan-Moor Corp.

1

Space Glossary

EMC 3349 • © Evan-Moor Corp.

4

Space Glossary

EMC 3349 • © Evan-Moor Corp.

3

Space Glossary

EMC 3349 • © Evan-Moor Corp.

6

Space Glossary

EMC 3349 • © Evan-Moor Corp.

5

Space Glossary

EMC 3349 • © Evan-Moor Corp.

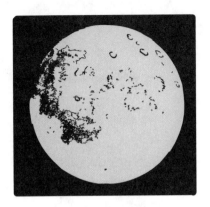

moon
(moon)

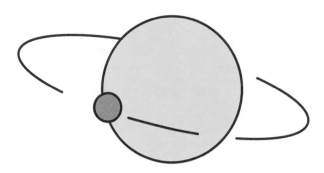

orbit
(**or**-bit)

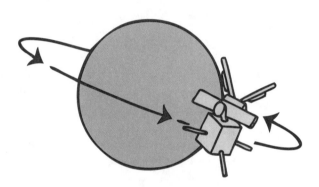

satellite
(**sat**-uh-lite)

meteor
(**mee**-tee-ur)

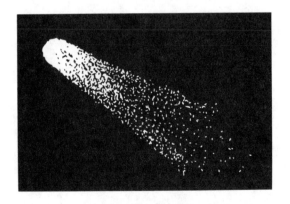

comet
(**kom**-it)

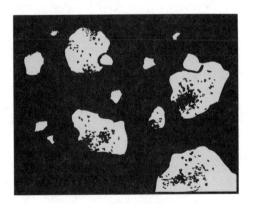

asteroid
(**as**-tuh-roid)

8

Space Glossary

EMC 3349 • © Evan-Moor Corp.

7

Space Glossary

EMC 3349 • © Evan-Moor Corp.

10

Space Glossary

EMC 3349 • © Evan-Moor Corp.

9

Space Glossary

EMC 3349 • © Evan-Moor Corp.

12

Space Glossary

EMC 3349 • © Evan-Moor Corp.

11

Space Glossary

EMC 3349 • © Evan-Moor Corp.

Space Glossary

1. meteor
2. sun
3. comet
4. planets
5. galaxy
6. orbit
7. Milky Way
8. star
9. satellite
10. asteroid
11. moon

$\dfrac{o}{1}\dfrac{u}{}\dfrac{r}{}\;\dfrac{s}{2}\dfrac{o}{3}\dfrac{l}{4}\dfrac{a}{5}\dfrac{r}{6}\;\dfrac{s}{7}\dfrac{y}{8}\dfrac{s}{9}\dfrac{t}{10}\dfrac{e}{}\dfrac{m}{11}$

SPACE GLOSSARY

Lift the flap to check your answers.